THE FACE OF JACK MUNRO

OTHER BOOKS BY TOM WAYMAN

Waiting for Wayman, 1973
For and Against the Moon: Blues, Yells and Chuckles, 1974
Money and Rain: Tom Wayman Live!, 1975
Free Time, 1977
A Planet Mostly Sea, 1979
Living on the Ground: Tom Wayman Country, 1980
Introducing Tom Wayman, 1980 (USA)
The Nobel Prize Acceptance Speech, 1981
Counting the Hours: City Poems, 1983

Editor

Beaton Abbot's Got the Contract, 1974
A Government Job at Last, 1976
Going for Coffee, 1981

Essays

Inside Job: Essays on the New Work Writing, 1983

The Face
of Jack Munro

TOM WAYMAN

HARBOUR PUBLISHING LTD

Published by
Harbour Publishing
Box 219 Madeira Park, B.C.
V0N 2H0

Design: Stephen Osborne
Cover: Gaye Hammond
Typesetting: Baseline Type & Graphics Cooperative
Printed & Bound in Canada

Publishing Assistance: Canada Council

Canadian Cataloguing in Publication Data
Wayman, Tom, 1945-
   The face of Jack Munro
Poems. ISBN 0-920080-59-6
I.Title. PS8595.A9F3 1985   C811'.54   C85-091488-4
PR199.3.W39F3 1985

Acknowledgements can be found on the last page.

CONTENTS

A PRAIRIE OF LIGHT

9 A Reason
10 December Letter to Pier Giorgio Di Cicco in Toronto
11 Forrie, O'Rourke, Penner, Sorestad
13 Suburban Pedagogy
13 Snowing
14 Road Songs
17 Giving Another Reading: Jasper Park
17 Articulating West

YOUR CLOTHES HAVE EXPERIENCES YOU KNOW NOTHING ABOUT

23 Raising a Relationship
24 Your Clothes Have Experiences You Know Nothing About
25 Sorting the Trash
27 Sleep
28 Nuclear Hockey
30 Lecture
31 Virus
33 Silos
35 Nationalism In No Way
36 The Music in the Silos
37 The Meadow
38 Enough
39 Paper
40 Mike

OPUSCULUM PAEDAGOGUM—A LITTLE WORK THAT TEACHES

45 Hammer
45 Surplus Value Poem
48 Bosses
49 The Sound: Factory System Poem
51 The Tongues
52 Surplus Value: Chalk White

53   Job Security
54   Holding the Line
56   Vest
56   Paper, Scissors, Stone
58   Bigfoot
61   Surplus Value: Interest
64   The Drawer

MOUNTAIN IN IT

69   Introductory
70   Dream of the Generals
82   Arboreal
83   Nuance
85   Breath: for Fred Wah
86   Country Feuds
88   Salmonwater
89   Wood
90   Motion Pictures
91   The Town Where Time Takes His Holidays
93   Broken Toes
95   Students
96   Why You Only Got "B Plus"
98   Wayman Among the Administrators
100   Uplands
101   East Kootenay Illumination
102   Saving the World
104   Monashee

THE FACE OF JACK MUNRO

107   The Hands
107   Meeting
109   Beetle
111   The Face of Jack Munro
123   In the Traitors' Season

A PRAIRIE OF LIGHT

A REASON

Driving fast in March
through the high, cold valley of the Athabaska
past Jasper,
I see men
lying out on the ice.

This lake has four or five men
bundled in sleeping bags
atop air mattresses or foam.
They lie face down, as though staring into the ice.
The next lake has two, with one man standing between them
whose eyes follow the cars as we speed
by a couple of pickups parked
just off the highway.

But the figures out on the ice
continue to lie face down.

Beyond the lakes, the mountains
are a stone backdrop in the sunshine.
And I think:
there is a reason
these men are here—fishing, perhaps,
though there are no poles or tackle boxes visible
and why they have to remain
looking into the ice
I can't guess. But then
what do I understand of these mountains
—their shapes familiar from the highway,
or a summertime hike in a safe corner?
The road, on the other hand, I am sure of
but what do I know about how asphalt is made
or how to set the timing on this car?

And yet I drive
staring over the steering wheel at the Rockies

and at men lying motionless
on the frozen water.

DECEMBER LETTER TO PIER GIORGIO DI CICCO
IN TORONTO

I love your poems about the villages' white walls
in the noon light, Giorgio,
about Arezzo, and your poem with the Tuscan cypresses
in which I appear as some kind of Canadian.
My friend, I write to you from this Edmonton winter
to say: forget that my family has been here so long,
these generations, forget the English name
my grandfather took in the British Army—
when you look at my face
you see a nose that means something, that was designed large
to draw in the rich odours of a Mediterranean wind,
that spreads out like a fisherman's sail
to catch the sun under a hot, cloudless sky.

My friend, I and this nose
have travelled many times across this continent
and we know a place where you and I will feel at home.
On the south coast of California, there are towns
the tourists pass through, that drowse in the heat,
where even this month the air is filled with the scent of
eucalyptus, with the spices of near-tropical flowers,
where lime and lemon
grow beside the stairs. At night when the traffic dies,
the sounds of the ocean wash in,
and you can stand for a moment listening
at the door.

      I have friends there, Giorgio,
who will be happy to see us,
pouring the warm California wine
and making the evening dance with poetry and music.
Let us go. We will settle into cottages
where a bougainvillaea is growing in the yard,
with jade plants and a palm
by the empty mailbox.

        And in the end

we will marry women
who never heard of Canada, and have children
who never heard of snow.

FORRIE, O'ROURKE, PENNER, SORESTAD

As wheat is gathered together
or the buildings that now rise
beside the South Saskatchewan,
one morning these four began
to instruct at the same city school.

But along with some others
who work in classrooms
these four are dazzled by words
—in their case, especially words
written by Canadians. And these four,
like secretly alcoholic teachers,
sat up nights plotting how to smuggle
certain books past the unsuspecting curriculum.
They hid poems in desk drawers
and stashed novels in the art room cupboards
until like a drunk who no longer cares
and finally hauls out a bottle
before his horrified class
these four reached for the words
as often as they could: reading the sounds
into sixty patient ears,
mimeographing the words and having their students
consider and discuss and write about them,
scheming to get more of the words
into the school library
and even making arrangements
so those who wrote the words
could one day stand in front of the classes
to speak the words themselves.

Now, not having been a student of theirs

I couldn't say how it is
to face these four through each long hour,
how hard they mark, what methods they use
to keep order. In my experience
the best that schools offer
when you are in them
is to finish and get out; it is years afterwards
what was said makes sense, if ever:
that you become grateful for
what this teacher introduced you to,
a chance remark that one made.
Thus these four learned
there are no thanks from the principal,
the school board is less than indifferent,
the parents never know what is going on
and writers
are always dissatisfied.
The students, meanwhile,
continue to be students:
accepting everything or rejecting everything
but forever in a hurry
to race out into real life and discover
it is largely more of the same.

So it is only the words
that can thank them, the way words do:
giving back to people the emotions
people show them
—here, a kind of drunken love
like a sort of song, so whatever these four do,
in school or out,
there is a music in them
and they sing

SUBURBAN PEDAGOGY
for Glen S.

The breeze winding in from the prairie
rustles the backyard grasses.
Sitting outside, we talk of gardens
and my friend points to the poplar
he planted fifteen years ago:
today several inches around at the base
and thirty feet tall.
A maple half its size
grows in a flower bed along a fence.
"Of course, the big one won't last
another ten years," my friend says.
"Poplar grow quickly, but have a short life span.
The maple will be here a long time yet."

I look up into the poplar leaves
in the wind. When I was younger
nothing was more stable
than a tree. In the sea-wind, men
could hack them down,
saplings grew, but a plant like this
always had been there,
and would stand.

Now I know what it means to age.
After a while, you are wiser than some trees.

SNOWING

Snow falls onto snow
this afternoon.

There is snow on the ice
under the logs of a footbridge
at the edge of a lake

where a creek also covered with snow
winds out of the woods.

In history, nothing is beautiful
except some ideas.

ROAD SONGS

1

Descending from Canmore, at the gate
of the Rockies, dropping toward
Calgary, and dusk. The freeway
curves from between the huge stones
that are these mountains, east to
the long rise and fall
of land, flattening
to plains. In the new darkness:
lamps of the city
spread over their hills
until my car
is among them. I find the correct interchange
and turn north.

   The radio
gives me a rock station,
its sound constant
while the city fades.
With me now are only lane markers,
clearance lamps of the trucks ahead
and headlights of faster cars
passing from behind beneath the black
sky, and its stars.

   Music
fills the car. Wheels
and the odometer spin, once more
I am out on this continent

in a night alive with sound.
The bands, the car models change
yet this beat has accompanied me
how many different places, to how much joy.
A year ago, riding I-5 south with a friend
after dark, beyond Bakersfield
we began to rise
into those mountains, the brooding highway
widening lane after lane
to our right, the trucks moving sideways
into these as we ascend.
Sudden eddy of lights
of a settlement off in the hills
or near the road: oil company signs
still burning as we roll by
on the level a few miles,
then climb again.
But past the crest, traffic
heavier, the radio picking up
the LA stations, we increase
speed as we start to fall, small towns appearing and
vanishing faster, then a city
spread out under us, no,
only a town, faint shapes of hills

and then a prairie of light
far as any horizon
racing toward us—street lamps, exit signs,
buildings close in on both sides
of the bright interstate,
the radio shrieking, hot autumn air,
scent of flowers, and the sea

where somebody else drives this evening
two thousand miles
over the curve of the world,
hearing this same music
below these stars

2

I am wheeling a Ford truck
with a loaded twenty-foot box
west through the mountains long after sunset:
hunched over the controls
seat jouncing with the uneven road
as it twists up
the curves and grades. The truck
fills its half
of the two-lane blacktop,
sluggish with this load,
ready to drift, so I have to be alert
each second
to hold the heavy vehicle
to its side, lowering the headlamps
at any traffic
then jabbing the foot switch
to high beam again,
the lights swaying through the blackness
watching for turns, for the road's edge
and the tiny flame of an animal's eyes.

Then the moon
sails out, full,
between two peaks
invisible before this instant:
the moon showing me
an embankment ahead, and the dark trees
rushing by either lane. The moon
on its unseen cold path
in space, and I here shifting down
to meet another rise,
the weight of the truck
on my shoulders, my arms
resting on the wide wheel
pushing down past gears, the loud engine,
the tires
that pound uphill on the earth
as it too

moves through the night: one more vehicle
pulling me through time

GIVING ANOTHER READING: JASPER PARK

After drinking for hours, sick
of my own voice
still talking,
at last I leave the Lodge and
head into the night air
back to my cabin

but like an image
of the power that heals,
a herd of deer
have come down from the forest in the darkness
and stand silently, some grazing,
on the cabin lawn.

ARTICULATING WEST

In May
I shook the prairie dust
out from under my tires
and took the route
over the Kicking Horse
and Rogers Pass,
meeting wet snow once
that day high in the forest,
and once hail,
until, descending,
at
Revelstoke
I ran into green:
the twelve different shades of green

and of yellow
in the springtime woods—
alder trees, the ferns and underbrush
and even fresh green
on the tips of the evergreen spruce.
And I rolled down the highway
filling my lungs with
the good green air, until near Sicamous
I turned off to follow the Shuswap River
deeper into the green: along that road
the lilac was in violet blossom
and the apple in white blossom
and each green farm
tucked in among the green hills
had its small orchard
of peaches or cherries.
And the green interior
of my green car
began to sprout: little woody shoots
appeared on the dashboard
and winding out of the handbrake handle,
tendrils and stalks and unfolding leaves
poking out of the glove compartment
and around the edges of the floor mats.
The steering wheel in my fingers
started to have the feel of fibre
and through the leaves now framing
the windshield
I could see the front of the car
disappearing into foliage.
Everywhere around me in the vehicle
plastic and metal
were becoming earth; the empty seat beside me
was now a flower bed
with roses and rhododendrons
about to open.
But the car's ride
began to be rough
and I poked my head through the laurel hedge

growing up the outside of the door
and saw the tires were no longer rubber
but looked more like tree trunks
forming around the spinning axles.
Thus, as I pulled into Vernon
the motor by this time halting and uneven too
I only just managed to locate John Lent's house
and turn up his driveway
where at the foot of his great green lawn
the entire construction that had been an automobile
stopped, and the sides
fell away like a cracked flowerpot
so I was left sitting
in a pleasant arbour
the stem of a young tree in my hand
and here were John and Jude coming smiling down the lawn
and all I could say
by way of explanation
was:
I'm home.

YOUR CLOTHES HAVE
EXPERIENCES YOU KNOW
NOTHING ABOUT

RAISING A RELATIONSHIP

It starts as two people enjoying themselves.
Months later, one of them gets a bit moody
and the other asks: "What's wrong?"
"Nothing," the first replies
but the other insists: "That's not true."
Then the first says: "I wasn't certain to begin with
but now I am. I checked and
whether you like it or not
we're having a relationship."
A silence. The first again:
"Of course, if you don't want to
I can always get rid of it."
A longer silence. Then the other:
"No, it's just. . . rather unexpected. But,"
cheering up,
"if you think about it,
it's marvellous." The two embrace
and life continues almost as before.

Except slowly the responsibility involved
becomes evident. One of the pair
out for a night on the town
decides to cut the evening short
because the other is home alone with the relationship.
Arguments now must be settled
with a minimum of fuss
for the relationship's sake.
Purchases are made on this basis, too.
"Let's go to Hawaii in December.
That'll be good for the relationship."
Various people aren't seen as often
due to their negative influence on the relationship.

And should the couple separate
there's the problem of custody.
Often one wants to keep it
and tries to convince the other to show more interest

though they are living apart.
Or, neither wishes it around in their new lives
and their friends become concerned
at how breezily the two fend off questions
about what happened to it.
Sometimes both would like the relationship
but don't want to be with each other
— which leads to a lot of confusion
as they attempt to sort this out.
Such uncertainty can drag on
until the relationship grows up and leaves on its own,
determined after all these years
to have some fun.

YOUR CLOTHES HAVE EXPERIENCES YOU KNOW NOTHING ABOUT

Clothes do not share your life
as fully as it might seem.
These companions surround me,
go where I go, even endure
the same weather.
Yet once they have been close
for even a morning
clothes become a chore:
laundry to me, but to them
a significant occurrence.
They are crammed into an odourous bag
next to something on which mud has dried
or which smells of bar smoke and noise.
After a week or more of this
they are suddenly dunked
into cold or scalding soapy water,
then swirled
dizzily, around darkness,
then faster

until they are conscious only that in some spinning canister
a thick grey liquid
is driven out of them amid incredible heat.
Wilted, bedraggled
they are hauled back into daylight
to be pressed flat by the burning heaviness
of an iron. At last they are returned
to rest on a hanger in a closet
to recuperate, or are folded away in a quiet drawer.
They aren't certain if they may wait just a few hours
before being put on
or will be neglected for months, seasons,
or if fashion or chance declares them unacceptable
they may never be worn again.

Despite their involvement in such events
I don't participate in
and so never entirely understand
they and I can provide each other
mutual assistance and comfort.
But though your clothes appear to be
a second skin,
their lives
are not ours.

SORTING THE TRASH

After four or five hundred
months of activity, the mind
becomes stuffed
with bundled newspapers,
salvaged two-by-fours, snow tires
from a car sold years ago,
half of a pair of ski poles.
On benches and in cupboards
are clothespins, broken drill bits,

empty spools, garden shears that need sharpening
and dozens of prescriptions
for ailments long forgotten.

One day a resolution is adopted
to sort out
what has accumulated: retaining some objects
and getting rid of the rest.
A small fire is lit
at the edge of the brain
and piece by piece the refuse
is dragged to the blaze.
As more debris is cleared away
the extent of the chore
becomes apparent. Each article shifted
discloses dozens of others
behind and underneath it.
What promised to be several hours work
now stretches into a weekend
and then a full time job
with fires burning several places at once.

The only external signs
of this task
result when the flames occasionally flare up
to singe the roots of a hair.
Outside the skull
that hair turns grey,
and then another,
as, strand by strand, indications of
the assessment
of an entire life
are revealed.

SLEEP

Sleep is a poor employee.
An executive can be busy all day
dealing with a dozen complex problems:
making decisions on some,
completing memos on others
and delegating further studies on more.
The day can run like clockwork—
everything occurring when it should
or nearly, appointments met on time,
each file in its place.

But when this person lies down
and asks for sleep
he gets the bad news: sleep hasn't punched in today.
Sleep seems to care nothing
for the wage system or the factory system;
he stays in bed late,
doesn't show up when he is supposed to,
wanders around
or just goofs. Anger
doesn't scare him, he can't be threatened
or hurried, he is sure he isn't going to be fired.
He usually performs okay when he does appear,
yet he sets his own hours and conditions
and won't budge. He is like an old mechanic
at a garage in the boondocks
when a big Cadillac passing by
breaks down and is towed in. He'll fix it
but when he wants to. You can't bribe him
or impress him, he belongs to another order
than urban corporate man or woman.
Sleep is the living embodiment
of the old ideal:
decide for ourselves down at the union hall
the terms we agree to work under
and display them there; if the owners
want to learn the details

they have to come to us.
Plus: no haggling. Take it or leave it.
If the owner balks,
it's a strike.

          The only known technique
to coerce sleep
is to drug him, and drag him to his post.
But like anyone, he doesn't produce well
stoned, his heart isn't in it,
he does a shoddy job. Sleep
seems to be part of the past
or the future; he has never recognized
the Industrial Revolution,
still muttering every night
about a better way to live.

NUCLEAR HOCKEY

Thirty-five thousand
people
assemble in Kitsilano Park—on sidewalks,
grass, parking lots
and the streets, clutching cardboard signs,
leaflets, banners, spare clothing
and beginning to discard the paper, portions of artifacts
and unused bits of food
left whenever human beings gather.

Children and adults push through the crowd
of other adults and children, searching
for friends, or relatives they are supposed to meet.
A haze of noise hangs over us
as we wait to start: much talk
and some musical instruments,
shouts, a radio, and car engines along adjacent boulevards.

This will be a walk which the organizers say
is against nuclear war.
But there are people here opposed to all wars
or in favour of peace:
some pro or con one of these concepts
as a way of defining who they are,
others present as a duty
to a friend, or because of one feeling they have
among many.

                And some weeks from now
a gathering equally large
will also parade over Burrard Bridge to Sunset Park,
this time to honour
the municipal hockey team:
fans. As at today's march
people will invent slogans, chants,
will prepare homemade posters and banners,
will debate tactics and strategy, predict future occurrences,
devise and wear costumes
—then, somebody dressed as the Stanley Cup;
this day, a middle-aged man in a chef's outfit
and constantly quizzical expression
who carries a model rocket adorned with US and Russian flags
on a serving tray, with a sign attached to his apron:
who ordered this A-bomb?

Both these marches took place
because citizens
want to win,
want to influence those active in determining
what is going to happen,
want, if they could, to decide
what will occur.

But some events
are not susceptible to
the wishes of men and women:

votes, or democracy
do not seem to be a factor.

So a walk like this
is a hope, a petition to God,
is publicity, is a sense of
how many agree, is information.

Such a march is not
choice, is not participation, not change:
it is not yet freedom.

LECTURE

We sit in rows
facing a man
who is talking. We
are not saying anything.
Suddenly a door near the back
opens
and most of us turn our heads.

Is someone
from a
different life
about to enter?
Will he or she bring
the air from outside
tasting of the sea,
spices and malt,
fresh-cut planks?
Will it be a person
who can articulate
why we are uneasy
in this room,
fearful of complaining

when what is said
is unsatisfactory?

Whoever is entering
is in the door now
and we observe
she is
only one of us,
nervous at arriving late,
hurriedly taking a seat.
Our heads
swivel again
silently to where the talker
has continued
with his words
all this time.
Maybe he
will deliver us, break
into song, reveal wonders,
make our presence in this
cramped room
worthwhile. But it looks
doubtful.

Toward the rear, a door opens.

VIRUS

Evolution has not ended.
Chance surges of radiation
continue to mutate genes,
freak combinations of cells
produce unusual configurations
in organisms that struggle to survive
and prosper.

In the constructions

women and men make, too,
new beings
try to adapt. There is a virus
which has spread
and now flourishes everywhere:
a living protein
which disorients those it infects
so they believe they are more important
than some other men and women
and that there are people
more worthy than themselves.
This illness at present is
epidemic; a majority of us
have contracted a type of it.
To the disease we give up
our ability to reason, decide and act
together
to benefit ourselves and each other.
Those persons most strongly affected
ascend the hierarchical chains of control
the virus creates
and feeds on
contrary to all ecological sense.
For how could a structure be more impractical
than top-down direction,
rule by the sickest? These individuals
become obsessed with confirming their position
and with being rated by those above them
as ill enough to rise to the next link of command.
Yet such women and men
are not born with the disease
or the power it grants them.
In our delirium
we transfer to these people
all we might be.

                    A cure
is unknown, though attempts constantly are made
to develop antibodies

on a small scale—the level at which resistance
has had the greatest success.
But many victims, hazy with fever,
become disinterested
and accept their condition as normal.
A number of the sick
turn shrill, proclaiming time
is running out, that no species so infected
can long withstand much stress.
The resilience of the host, though,
cannot be measured. We are sure only
that this virus
turns us against one another,
stunts us,
weakens us. And the prognosis
does not look good.

SILOS

Chemical rain
stings the oil-flecked surface of the sea.

Inland, a strip of forest infected by blight,
dyed orange with a retardant

dropped by helicopter,
surrounds a sterile lake.

Here the silos
are emplaced.

Inside these, below ground, men
with the faces of machines

forget everything they learned about the sun,
leaf through manuals filled with initials and

numbers, searching for the coded designations for
death. They have brothers under the ocean

in submersible cylinders
holding more of the burning fodder

meant to feed death. And above
in the ultraviolet sky

is the remote thunder of airborne silos
packed with electronic delivery programs

for the fertilizers of death.
Yet bears

still walk our forest paths
down each evening

to the landfill, browsing
among the crushed tins and papers, disposable diapers,

the abandoned televisions.
Deer lie along the highway ditches

near portions of robin, porcupine, grouse
on the pavement. Our masters

have established their rights to the earth:
gut it, package and sell it

and get out. In their humming silos
they store what they save

of this harvest
as if to ensure no report of themselves,

of what they do
passes into any history. And they ask us

to help improve the planet, they urge us
don't litter

NATIONALISM IN NO WAY

contributes to human freedom.
Is there any country
without some individual who claims
to have been selected to represent the nation
or some important segment of it?
And we're supposed to conclude
that thus whatever he
(this person is almost always a he)
does and says and believes is more significant
than how other people act or speak or think.
As a consequence, a number of citizens
leap into the gap between
this exalted person and the rest of us.
These bureaucrats, sycophants, enforcers
try to grab for themselves a spot on the ladder
leading from us to the top.
They announce they can administer, guide
and otherwise interpret
we poor souls who are "represented."
Naturally, a certain amount of
violence—internal and external—
is necessary to ensure the continuation
of this arrangement.

The nation-state is one step in the development
of the human species. But so is
a suit of armour.
And that's what these countries actually are:
a suit of armour into which we get jammed.
It's stifling in here
and the suit, though kept more or less in working order
so it appears about as efficient as when new
five hundred years ago,
is obsolete, cumbersome
and offers a view through the holes in the helmet
only of a row of other suits of armour,
iron instead of people, hard and

threatening,
with nearly all aspects of their construction and use
intended for war.

THE MUSIC IN THE SILOS

Cylindrical arks
sit and steam,
locked away
from the rain.
Electrons race
through their tubular
superstructure.
Men and women
have put death
in these, and also
money
and what that money didn't
buy: music,
braces for teeth,
geography text books,
a vacuum cleaner
for subway stops.
The arks carry
rice,
convalescent
sun rooms, and
paint. Nothing alive
is within, however,
no crow or dove
can leave to
find
firm ground
and return.
There is no known way
to open the arks
to remove

the possibilities
they contain.
And once they are lofted
onto the
waters
all that can be
unloaded
from them
is
death.

THE MEADOW

At the end of summer
on the highway south
just after sundown, the sky still bright

but with a haze
from the slash burning
all along the North Thompson

or perhaps from the air's coolness
—like a window open into the autumn

I passed a meadow
where the thin smoke or mist
hung over the grass in the chill light
and some trees
with the mountain close behind

and I wanted to say
to my dead:
"There is still mist
on the meadow
you would think beautiful.
Here is a place
you are, for me.
And after me,

what can we care
what those we don't know
remember?"

A meadow
on the road to Kamloops;
early evening.

ENOUGH

"Se trata de que tanto he vivido
que quiero vivir otro tanto."
—*Pido silencio*

Like Neruda, I want to write so much
that after I'm dead my voice goes on speaking
everywhere, and they have to shut my books
to get some peace and quiet.

Unlike Neruda, alas,
already my books have begun to fly away.
I don't know what else I expected
on this mortal planet: nothing persists.

Even if some of my poor poems were to remain
in print, I worry about the rest.
And what about the ones I never tried to publish,
or those I invented in my head
but lost before I got them down on paper?
And more: the poems I still intended to write?

Plus, the help I could give my words in person
—the inflections, pauses, my generous gestures—
cannot survive: the printed letters
are only the tombstones
where how I uttered the words are buried,
just as the published poems

are the graveyards of what I meant to say.
A graveyard may have certain uses for the living
but not usually for very long.
And after that, except for a few historians
why would anybody alive want to visit them?

Like everyone, I came out of silence
and go into silence.
And unlike lots of others
I got to talk plenty while I was here.
So when I finally stop
—much to some people's relief—
I should agree
that's enough.

But. . .

PAPER

Anything put down on paper
becomes two-dimensional.
If an effect of depth is created
this is an illusion.
Paper makes whatever is said on it
very smooth and thin.

Paper starts with a blank expression
and seldom attains much intelligence.
It is as willing, whether fresh and empty
or covered with vital orbital equations,
to drift away on a gust of wind, slip behind a desk
or catch fire under the right circumstances.

Paper can have power
—money, stocks, orders—
but does not act itself. Aloof, indifferent,

it is the perfect official.
It does not like to be crinkled or stained
in public; it tries to show itself as refined
even when it has to earn a living.
Paper reveals exactly what it has been instructed to say
despite any of its own experiences.
It may offer hints
of another message
but nothing that would stand up in court.

Paper usually presents the world
as black and white. Where it suggests colour,
most people conclude the shades are not accurate.
Paper edits, omits,
compresses complexity into a rectangle.
Around it, the universe swirls with other forms,
hues, emotions, movement
and sound.
Anything on paper
is a lie.

MIKE

A man who knows how to fix things:
at work, staring into a machine
to determine how well two metals bond
he understands
what here is the fault of an improper adjustment
of the instrument, what is the result of
poor specimen preparation,
or whether the whole procedure needs to be repeated
at a different temperature or pressure.
Off work, he lives amid the constant appearance
of damaged toasters, lamps,
washers, stoves
—his own, and what friends bring him:

pulling a Volkswagen engine
because of oil on the clutch plate
and replacing that, or locating the trouble
in a TV set as the on-off-volume switch
and then disassembling the switch, too.
If you have to sum him up:
a child of his is taken to hospital
after a fall once
but the nurses tell him the X-ray is out of order.
He explains he uses these
in his work with minerals, and so
he settles down to repair the X-ray device
to enable the hospital to begin
fixing his child.

Over the years, his mind
has become like a wholesale hardware supply firm—
where the counter clerk can not only show you
the latest in plastic piping
but is completely familiar with the genealogy
of replacement faucet designs
and is pleased to relate the advantages and disadvantages
of Ford carburetors, GE pumps
or alternative techniques for welding.
Nothing human that is constructed
is foreign to him: if it went together
it can go wrong
but it also can be taken apart
and put right.
Like most such men, he usually works alone,
yet always conscious of the instant he has done all he can
without a particular tool belonging to a friend
or when an object must be referred to an expert
—meaning someone with technical data, repair procedures
or spare parts he doesn't have on hand.

In this life, then,
the broken things
seek him: his laboratory at work

filled with metal rods that snapped,
plastic strapping that gave way,
their owners on the phone to him to discover why.
At home, there is a wooden toy
on which the glue didn't hold for more than a week
and a relative anxious for him to examine
the ignition wiring on a tractor.

His daily achievements,
like everyone's with his abilities,
are a finger in the steadily crumbling dike
of our mechanical world.
But he
is not content with that,
also peering today
far down at the structure of certain atoms
to find out what's wrong with them.

OPUSCULUM PAEDAGOGUM
—A LITTLE WORK
THAT TEACHES

HAMMER

A hammer is rising. A hammer
thrown up at the end of the day by a carpenter
with blood on the handle where his blisters have been.
A hammer. It lifts as well on the wave of steam
pouring up from the pots of a kitchen — a tiny kitchen
of an apartment, and that of a restaurant
serving a hundred customers at once.

A great cry of tedium
erupting out of papers and fluorescent glass
carries the hammer higher. It goes up end over end
on a tune broadcast to a million people.
And it climbs
on the force of a man's arm alone
flung straight up from the sickness that is his life.
It rises out of the weight of a body falling.

Nothing can stop it. The hammer has risen for centuries
high as the eaves, over the town. In this age
it has climbed to the moon
but it does not cease rising everywhere each hour.
And no one can say what it will drive
if at last it comes down.

SURPLUS VALUE POEM

All day, metal curls up from the drill
or bends and falls from the shears
onto the cement floor. Grit from the files,
the sawn-off ends of bars,
rivets that failed, washers
and even sawdust that someone tracked in
from another department
lie underfoot. When we're parts short
or otherwise have to look busy

or in any case before the last hooter
somebody grabs a broom and gathers
what we have discarded
into a pile, then onto
an old piece of cardboard
and into a waste can.

                    Then
if it's the end of the day,
we take off our coveralls,
go wash up
and spend the last minutes of the shift
peering from our area out at the time clock,
lunchboxes under our arm,
to make sure no one from another department
gets there ahead of us.
Suddenly somebody with the acutest of senses
of the inner workings of a clock
starts the dash, and a half-second later
when the hooter resounds
there's already a long line,
everyone urging those in front
to hurry it up, while a few deals are proposed
I got coffee for you yesterday.
So punch out for me today, will you?
and resolved *Screw off,* or
accepted *Okay, but tomorrow*
you punch out for me.
Then the clock efficiently stamps your card
like the good bureaucrat it is.
And meanwhile the next shift is coming in.
And the PA is busy trying to redeem itself
for the past eight hours, and now insists
there is another world out there, announcing
Phone calls for Ken Smith, for Johnny Kurchak,
Archie Pierce. The PA follows you
to the parking lot, and if it's anyone we know
there's a certain amount of kidding *Hey, it's your wife,*
Billy. She must have found out.
Then the tangle of cars

at the lot gate, and the next second
you're heading home. Whether you made production
or not, whether it all went smoothly
or not, it's done for another day
and anyway it wasn't your fault
and even if it was
there's nothing you can do about it now.

    In the plant
the guys from Maintenance carry the waste cans
out to the yard
and empty them into the bins: the shavings and
scraps from fabrication and assembly,
plus the worn ribbons and botched papers
from the office. At this moment,
as the next shift starts,
the security guards
drift over to stand by the bins.
For the trucks that arrive to pick up
what fell away from each hour we worked
have armoured sides.
As these move out of the plant
and along the avenues, the police
keep a casual eye on them, ready at any sign of trouble
to speed to their aid. The trucks
pull in not at the junkyards,
but at a bank
and when they leave from there
they haul only thin white envelopes
to be delivered
at the homes of certain men
from the executive offices, and those of other people
who never go near the plant.
Something taken out of the hours we work
they cherish; what we throw away
and never miss
makes them rich. The money they get
is like another deduction
on our cheque each Friday,

one that isn't listed
so we don't complain.

But it keeps us
what we are.

BOSSES
after Nicanor Parra

The boss who stands behind you
watching you work.
The boss who orders you to look busy.
The boss who insists:
"I'm sure I told you to do that."
The boss who, after you've made nine trips
carrying an extra heavy load of boards,
sees you walking with a light load
and directs your foreman to tell you to work harder.

The foreman who can't resist showing you a better way.
The foreman who won't let you
do something a better way.
The one who is also head
of the union's grievance committee.
The foreman who is unable or forgot to
requisition enough parts
and orders you to "make do with what you have."

The supervisor who is afraid
of the boss.
The supervisor in love with memos.
The supervisor who checks the washroom
to be certain no one is there too long.
The new supervisor who doesn't understand what is happening
and so concentrates on enforcing regulations
everybody forgot about years ago.

These bosses
in their coats and ties,
with their specially-coloured hard hats,
their offices, watches, clipboards,
with their ulcers
and their pathetic attempts to appear calm

are, by and large,
totally useless.

THE SOUND: FACTORY SYSTEM POEM

The moment the hooter goes
I reach for the small cardboard case in my tool box
and tear off a tuft of cotton
to plug in each ear.

Before the shift starts,
in the low sounds of people clocking in,
getting changed and standing around drinking coffee
and talking, or reading the paper, the first aid man
puts a dozen new packages of ear cotton
on a table in his room
for anybody who has run out.

If I don't use it, the noise
doesn't seem so bad at the start
with rivets being hammered, the hiss of
air hoses, the shouts, engines, the pounding.
Yet as the first hours pass, the sound
begins to echo in my ear:
never deafening
but a steady high-pitched drilling
I'm always aware of.

Even with the cotton
I touch my ear to make sure the plugs are in place

when a router or winch seems especially loud.
The fibre
itches a little constantly
but if I take it out for a second
when I put the cotton back it's like on a hot day
when you dive under the surface of a sunlit lake
into the cool and quiet.

                    Speech
is audible almost unchanged:
people making suggestions, or jokes,
and what the foreman says to do next.
Occasionally I have to ask someone to talk louder, though.
A few guys wear Mickey Mouse ears—the headphones
which function the same as cotton.
But since the Company doesn't provide these
most of us stick with what we're given.

Yet if they could make an ear protector
so powerful that when we wore it
there was absolute silence,
a voice
would still speak continually here in the din
saying:

        a factory is not a tool
for production, like a screwdriver
or the compressed air impact wrench.
It is a way of organizing people
to do a job, human beings
who are supposed to follow orders
and not argue, perform
and not comment. There can be no such thing as
a socialist factory
any more than a left-wing, interest-charging bank
or a Red army. These structures, hierarchies
belong to another age
and have to be altered, dismantled, rebuilt
to improve them

for as long as they can't be shut down.
But they will never
be ours.

THE TONGUES

On this job, it is the tongues that work.
Legs and arms and the trunk function
to convey the tongue from place to place.
The tongue grows fat at its labour,
lolling in its socket filled with saliva:
the more it exercises
the grander it swells, while the fluid around it
turns slowly to oil, or grease.

By the end of each afternoon
the arms and fingers are weary
of holding up only papers
and food. The legs become stiff
with spending the hours as props
for the tongue. As recreation
the tongue enjoys meeting with other tongues,
all of them oscillating back and forth
discussing the issues of the day.
The bodies that carry them wait patiently
for them to finish.

One of the topics the tongues consider
is how pleasant it would be
to have arms and legs
completely under the tongues' control.
They agree these should be more quick-witted,
less contrary and sullen
than what serves them now.

SURPLUS VALUE: CHALK WHITE

The students wander into class
I wait by the door
and think of the fees they paid in September:
admission charges
to my act today,
to a whole term of performances.
Yet this show is also subsidized
by taxes: deducted from shifts the students worked
last summer, or the past few years,
plus everybody else's time
including the hours I am employed.
All this money
—suitably apportioned of course—
might be my salary.

Except

there's the building to pay for
and heat and light
and keep clean, and someone
to admit, counsel, record,
write letters, purchase supplies,
plan residences, hire and fire,
argue with the Ministry, invite the Mayor
to tour the premises . . .

So,

like the expensive office tower
of steel and glass
filled with men in suits
that rises from the work
of a young man on a sidehill
in the mud, kneeling to pull a choker cable
under a fallen spruce,
these people stand
on the back of my voice
in the seminar room now, on my papers

scrawled with my notes for today.
Among these men and women
is one who decided
he should receive twice my wages
for his work
and his secretary should get half
and the person who waxes the floor, half.
This man takes
from their work and mine
to fatten himself,
he seizes from the labour all of us do
—all equally necessary—
more cash for himself.
At the end of each month he hands me
an envelope
and announces: "This is what you're worth."
He says it at the end of each week
to the others employed here.

But this is not what we're worth.
This is not
what we earned.

JOB SECURITY

for Wayne Paquette

"Job security," he says,
"is not just another demand.
What our parents wanted
and their parents
was land reform. Not to become landlords
but because to own your forty acres
meant you would always eat," he says
in his mild Quebec accent
as we walk across the small campus
at the western tip of Montreal.
"Today with agribusiness

that isn't even an issue,"
he says.

      His thick hands
pass in the air: hands he took
through five years in a monastery,
then out of the Church to teach
philosophy—a life, he explains,
which made him feel removed
from his family,
leaving them behind,
until the day he understood himself
the same as his parents and sisters and brothers:
employed.

"They tell us they want to fix the economy,"
he says, "and then they'll think about jobs.
But they should start with the jobs,
then make the economy function.
That's the reform we need:
college or not,
to be sure of your job means to have
land under your feet."

HOLDING THE LINE

Eleven days that September
under umbrellas and vinyl raingear
the faculty are out to support
the custodians, library clerks,
secretaries on strike
for a new contract.
We clump together now and then
to exchange rumours about
how the talks are progressing, morale,
and who crossed. The slow four hour shifts
pass in the damp cold.
Occasionally a student

hurries through our line to seek the services
he or she wants to purchase.
On their return, some take the soggy leaflets
which detail our reasons
for being here,
others ignore us,
a few want to argue:
you'll never make back
the money you lose by striking.
"Figure it out," says Barb,
a steward.
"If I work another few years,
the increase we'll get more than pays
for these weeks. And if we don't ask
for more, they sure won't ever
raise our wages."

But these students intend
anger, not debate
and they head off along the street.

Then a Monday after supper
I get a phone call: "It's settled.
Classes as scheduled tomorrow.
Show up at eight ready to teach."
When I drive onto campus next morning
the rain has stopped.
I leave my car and walk back
to stand at the edge of the road
where we lived for days.
No one is here.
The picket signs have vanished; traffic
rushes by.
Nothing remains of our actions
except where, inside,
some people
go on
holding the line.

VEST

When a supervisor says *No*
you did that wrong

despite my
just-
ifications

you shouldn't have done it

I feel fastening around my ribs
a vest
of rage

whose tight clasp
restricts my chest, weights down
each breath

When did I cast
my ballot for this power
over my time, this vise
diminishing me

Outmoded
as a dunce cap

still in use

PAPER, SCISSORS, STONE

An executive's salary for working with paper
beats the wage in a metal shop operating shears
which beats what a gardener earns arranging stone.

But the pay for a surgeon's use of scissors
is larger than that of a heavy equipment driver removing stone
which in turn beats a secretary's cheque for handling paper.

And, a geologist's hours with stone
nets more than a teacher's with paper
and definitely beats someone's time in a garment factory with
     scissors.

In addition: to manufacture paper,
you need stone to extract metal to fabricate scissors
to cut the product to size.
To make scissors you must have paper to write out the specs
and a whetstone to sharpen the new edges.
Creating gravel, you require the scissor-blades of the crusher
and lots of order forms and invoices at the office.

Thus I believe there is a connection
between things
and not at all like the hierarchy of winners
of a child's game.
When a man starts insisting
he should be paid more than me
because he's more important to the task at hand,
I keep seeing how the whole process collapses
if almost any one of us is missing.
When a woman claims she deserves more money
because she went to school longer,
I remember the taxes I paid to support her education.
Should she benefit twice?
Then there's the guy who demands extra
because he has so much seniority
and understands his work so well
he has ceased to care, does as little as possible,
or refuses to master the latest techniques
the new-hires are required to know.
Even if he's helpful and somehow still curious
after his many years—
again: nobody does the job alone.

Without a machine to precisely measure
how much sweat we each provide
or a contraption hooked up to electrodes in the brain
to record the amount we think,

my getting less than him
and more than her
makes no sense to me.
Surely whatever we do at the job
for our eight hours—as long as it contributes—
has to be worth the same.

And if anyone mentions
this is a nice idea but isn't possible,
consider what we have now:
everybody dissatisfied, continually grumbling and disputing.
No, I'm afraid it's the wage system that doesn't function
except it goes on
and will
until we set to work to stop it

with paper, with scissors, and with stone.

BIGFOOT

Yeti, Sasquatch, Bigfoot: from the polar snows
to the desert, and on this continent
from Florida to British Columbia—
men and women who swear they glimpse
at the edge of their vision
in a clearing in the woods or on a trail
something tall or short
but always hairy, and leaving
a larger-than-normal footprint.

But the truth is
we live mostly in cities
where we are usually unremarkable.
Once a year, though,
like everyone we get some weeks off work
and we head for the country.
To us, it's important

to feel part of the Earth, so instead of using
campers, vans, all-terrain vehicles
we let our hair grow
(overnight, because holidays
don't last forever)
and stretch ourselves to our real human size
and run free.
We pick remote spots
so as not to bother local residents
or any of our motorized brothers and sisters
who might blunder this far into the weeds.
And when our time is up
we scrunch ourselves back
into wage earners
and trudge off Monday to punch in,
and hedge on questions about where we spent our vacation,
the inevitable argument starting
about whether Vegas or Disneyland is tops.

In town, only our feet
would betray us. Our feet won't shrink
as much as they should: I guess because
they are most in touch with the ground
during the rest of the year
even through concrete or steel.
So we wear special shoes, or work boots,
that curl the end of the foot
underneath, the back of the toes growing calloused
and the tendons of the foot strained
from hiding who we are.

How did this occur? For me
it began when I heard someone argue
I have a right to be alive at work:
I ought not to throw these hours of my life away.
The more I pondered this
the hairier I became
and my feet commenced swelling uncomfortably
as if to teach me

I had a long journey ahead.
At last a friend, similarly afflicted,
approached me about my appearance
and through him I met our tribe.

For we are everywhere. The name we prefer
is *bigfeet*, because there are women and men
from years before whose shoes we have to fill.
We don't all agree
on how to do this:
some of us meet in small groups
and debate theory,
others go up and down the line
in our painful boots trying to talk to people.
Like any tribe, we have our idiots,
our madmen, our traitors.
Yet even the worst of us
began with wanting a happier life
for himself or herself, which includes
all those around us.

Right now our numbers
are nowhere near what they should be.
Perhaps if you think hard enough
about what happens to you daily
you could become one of us.
It might be, like me, you can wonder
why work, or the rest of our life
isn't free and friendly and just.
Or why men and women treat each other
and the planet as they do.
If you find you can use additional thoughts
you could try reading some books
they haven't assured us since birth
are the correct ones to read
But you shouldn't have to go to such lengths.
And you'll know you're on the right track
when hair starts appearing
on fresh areas of your skin

and you feel an irresistible urge
to reach, and grow.
Most likely somebody close will be watching
and you will be contacted.
If you're completely isolated,
be careful the police don't notice you first.

But you probably won't worry about that.
You'll be concentrating on
seeking out the wild places
now and then to enjoy,
and struggling to create the successes and failures
as one by one
and together
the human race transforms conditions
until each of our hours
—like our new bodies—
is fuller, swifter, further ranging,
more at ease on the Earth.

SURPLUS VALUE: INTEREST

I slide my cheque to the teller.
She keys the numbers in, and months later
the computer adds more money to my account:
interest. While I wasn't looking
my dollars went out
and earned more dollars.
For these weeks
my money must have shut off its alarm clock each morning,
swung its legs over the side of the bed
and sat for a moment to clear the dreams from its mind.
It groaned and got up,
gulped some bacon and eggs and coffee
and stood in the dawn or rain
to wait for the bus. It spent all day

in the factory noise
meeting the others employed at that firm,
mastering a few complicated assembly procedures
and how to goof, learning which foremen are okay
and which meals the cafeteria
can't completely ruin. At the end of each week
it went straight to the bank.
At the teller's wicket
it signed over its pay
to me, except for a sizeable amount
the bank took
because the bank insists this is what it deserves
for helping my dollars secure employment.
Then my money left through the bank doors
with nothing in its pockets.
All it could do on the weekend
was sit in its room somewhere
until early Monday, when it stands at the bus stop again
reading the headlines in the newspaper vending machine.

But how can money work?
When I look at the figures
newly credited to my account
it is as though I received a cheque
from the corporation or mortgage holder
the bank loaned my dollars to.
It is as if *I* went to work for these people.
Except I can't recall
putting in those hours, breathing oil mist or diesel exhaust
or drafting letters and memos under fluorescent lamps
or trembling high up on an unsteady platform
of ladders and planks replacing somebody's siding.

So who did the work
for which I am paid?
And, in turn, when I am employed
who collects dollars that should go to me?
Who established this arrangement
out of my need to store my cash,

this mutual robbery none of us asked for
or got to vote on
but which we are expected to accept as an immutable
fact of nature
as organic as sunshine?

And who benefits?
What work did those who control the bank
complete, that they are handed cheques
on which are printed the seal of a company
or the name and address of folks
who borrowed my money?

Moreover, an illusion
appears. The numbers in my account
swell, but if I closely examine the digits
I discover each has diminished in size.
While we are forced to steal from each other
the worth of the portion we are permitted to hang onto
shrinks.

How much simpler the world would be
if we thought through this matter again.
Instead, we are urged to agree
this is the best possible structure
and to disturb it
would be to tamper
with forces we are advised no one can comprehend.

THE DRAWER

On each job, there's a drawer
in the superintendent's desk
or filing cabinets of the office manager
or at the foreman's station
which contains
amid pencil stubs
faded memos and directives
blank time cards
snapshots of people
who no longer work here
a pad of permission slips
to take your tools out of the plant for the weekend

our right

to determine how each shift
will feel:
the way the task will be divided
who works where
the sort of coordination
needed, if any
the quality of the finished product
the effect our employment
and that which we produce
has on people's lives
and more
and more—everything
that should be ours
because our daily existence
goes into this job
and hence we as free adults
have the right
to manage our work
together. To alter it, improve it
abolish it. What else could democracy mean?
For while this absent part of us is held
somewhere at the jobsite, what can't they do to us
off work?

When kings and queens reigned
they claimed divine, and hence natural, law
justified their privileges.
Now the owners argue
they risk their money in this enterprise
and thus they are entitled to establish the procedures
by which to control us here:
as if our contribution
—our thought and actions
and selves each day—
is worth less
than dollars.

But though what we lack
is jumbled inside a drawer
in the dark
with other objects considered peripheral
to the job
no one finds justice
by obtaining the key to the compartment
for herself or himself
or with the blessing of the company.
That which we are missing
is locked up
in the people we work with
and only through them
can we secure at last
what belongs to us
inside that drawer.

MOUNTAIN IN IT

for David Everest
and Judy Wapp

INTRODUCTORY

The mountains are not Selkirks
as the maps tell
              but *Kutenai* "people of the water"
the tribe
forced out of this valley
   pushed south and east
away from the Lake
              and River   with their name
where they canoed
for berries
and hunting
         in their season—
arrowheads, a few photos
                and gone

leaving their name
when prospectors moved north
           with the new century   miners
calling these forests
           Colorado
who built Silverton
           New Denver
                the British
owning the railroad, the smelter south
at Trail
     but the markets lay
across the line
further south
        to Spokane
and the Columbia

           Other English here
began orchards
         and gardens
in remittance colonies, retirement colonies
ready to keep
        an Empire
but civil war

broke out in Europe, 1914
                              and many left
to take part, some enlisting
                              as *Canadians*
whatever that was:
                        lakes and valleys
    west of the Rockies
                              ore in the earth   timber
cabins and small hayfields
                              against mountains
with other names

DREAM OF THE GENERALS

1

In Poland, the General sleeps.
The generals of my country sleep.
The General of Chile sleeps.
Each dreams
winter,
the generals' season,
this century's season.

    In these valleys, a wraith
    of whirling ice and snow
    spins through the passes.
    Whiteness covers the mountain peaks
    in the dark; the highway crews
    are out all night,
    yellow lights flashing on the graders,
    the sand trucks
    holding the road open
    in the storm.

At dawn
snow lies on the beaches,

on the lakeshore's rocks.
Snow circulates in the wind, blown
off the roofs of the houses in the woods,
boughs of the firs

into the world. Travellers by day
notice a blue light
under the snow, an intense blue
visible at the bottom of a hole
where one leg went down
nearly to the thigh, or in the cavity
the point of a ski pole makes, a deep blue
under the crust of the snow
the colour of
inside a rifle barrel,
the open eye of a general
who dreams.

        On the sides of cuts
the highway was built through,
water
forms long
frozen teeth.
By mid-afternoon
drops hang from the tip of each.
This is not the water of life.

2

When a general is created
a being out of an earlier era
appears,
a cockroach
suspended for generations in ice.

A general
wants every object to remain still
or move backward. Even death

is a matter the generals intend to decide.
Without their order
there shall be no harvest,
no planting, no mining.

To accomplish this, the generals pick
the young:
young men
who have been called *garbage*
until they are perfectly confident
and willing to obey. The generals are aware
the young lack time
to compare other lives, hopes, beliefs
besides what they are told.
The army is better than school
is what the young know.

> In cold sunlight
> the mountains beyond the Lake
> shine white, clear,
> ghastly.

A general understands
an army is for killing.
A general cannot strip down a diesel engine,
distinguish layers from meat birds,
erect a loafing barn, sharpen a chain saw.
A general's achievements
have no connection with democracy.
Which general has defended freedom for everyone
in his own country?
How much democracy does a general offer
those under his command?
What kind of freedom, then,
could a general ever protect?

And now the general's dream
has reached earth orbit, has chilled
the moon.

Yet the long haul driver
guides his tractor-trailer unit
over the icy roads,
pulling a cargo of cut-rate soft drinks
between the mountain towns
where men and women continue trying
to make of winter a home.

On the high pass between Salmo and Creston
a flagwoman in a parka
stops traffic while front-end loaders
remove the snow of a small avalanche
from the road. A pickup arrives to lead
the growing number of waiting cars and trucks
over the summit area.
Suddenly a shout comes down the line:
"Chain up! Chain up!"
And the drivers of the rigs
climb down from their cabs
to wrestle the metal links around the wheels.

The convoy begins to move through the snow.

3

In Poland, 1980,
a word was spoken against this season:
solidarity, the union of all
against the generals'
bosses.

It is not a new sound.
It was heard in this valley
in 1919, when the One Big Union
grew from people familiar with
the Industrial Workers of the World.
The IWW here by 1911
included municipal employees, teamsters

and many of the construction trades,
winning the eight-hour day in Nelson
"on all civic work, in lieu of
the nine-hour day."
And the IWW itself started
at Brand's Hall, Chicago, 1905,
with snow
deep on the sidewalks around the building
July 7, as William D. Haywood,
secretary-treasurer of the Western Federation of Miners,
spoke to the founding convention
This industrial union is an organization
that stands with the gates wide open
to take in every man and woman
and, if necessary, child that is working for wages
with either brain or muscle.
But let no one make a mistake.
While we are going to do everything we can to improve
and take advantage of every opportunity
offered to us to improve
the condition of the working classes as we go along,
the ultimate aim of this organization
is to get control of the supervision of industry.

> In Poland
> as at Winnipeg's 1919 OBU general strike,
> each glimpse of a better life for us
> takes this shape.
> What else could the vision consist of
> but this restless, organized unity?

In Poland, Solidarity
began with the shop committees
carrying the sound of the word
from plant to plant
and, after work, into homes
until the word
stood to ask
why do we need politicians and a government

besides
the democratic organization of where
we live and are employed?

The word
a path in the snow:

> Should freedom end
> the moment a person
> walks in a plant gate or the office door?
> Do we not have the right
> to be free citizens
> for the eight hours we work
> as well as the rest of the day?
> What is there about a smelter,
> planer mill, machine shop
> that excludes democracy from it forever
> in some people's minds?
> How is it those who assure us
> a factory can only be run as it is today
> don't work here in them?

A shovel, many shovels,
a bulldozer
labouring
to clear a road
in snow, to dig down
to the frozen soil
so light
can warm the ground. The word
is not about
what is written on paper, the dry hours
of conferences, commissions, the excitement
of rallies, tense moments of procedural maneuvers,
crowded halls of protest meetings,
but about
decisions made between the machines
when the line is halted
and among those unloading lumber,

and about generals —

waiting
or in power:

      the ice
      and the winter.

December 13, 1981:
darts of novocaine
on the freezing wind.
A knock on the door
after dark, Polish army trucks
selecting, gathering;
shots
on the avenues, at the shipyards
and mines, in detention camps:
the old season —
blood on the snow
blood on the snow.

Soldiers
to break the union,
break the strike,
to herd us
back on the job.

A soldier:
a lizard mauled by the cat
but still able to step delicately over the snow,
half its head torn away,
part of the face hanging,
blood visible on the top of its head
under the stars, pulsing
as the ribs puff out and are sucked in
spasmodically, the blood over the brain
expanding and contracting to that rhythm,
it steps,
it works,
it is alive.

Snow crumbling
on the edges of indentations
where boots have passed.

4

Don't tell us what is possible.
We have to determine what is right
and just, then how
to achieve this.

     In the larger plants
     a government poster tacked
     by the timeclock
     Be Sure To Register To Vote.
     But not
     about what happens to us here
     where the power of the nation,
     where even the generals' might
     is constructed,

     where winter
     is made.

A certain number of graves
per day, the production figures
of the generals.
The tons of snow
drifting down
         on the country.
And the police:
       icy sleet.

     "There seems to be something terrible
     in the Department of Highways system.
     None of the six mechanics at Highways
     knows who will do what until the next morning.
     Who will be sent away for parts, who
     will have to service a chain saw, who will help
     the welder. Just as the drivers won't know

whether they'll haul crush from Belgo to East Kelowna,
haul the dregs when the Gradall is sent out ditching
or spend the day waiting for their truck
to be serviced. No one knows.
There is no involvement of the worker
in the layout of work scheduling.
Sometimes there is something so obvious to be finished
everyone might expect to be assigned to a particular job.
Then the whole crew is sent elsewhere
to work at what seems totally unimportant.
For example, last year
we re-gravelled the highway shoulders by the airport
four times,
taking a week to complete it each time.

If they'd used pit-run—big rocks, gravel and boulders—
at first, it wouldn't have had to be done again.
But management said to use crush,
which is so fine it washes away whenever it rains.
And everybody—workers—was really upset about it
because it was so stupid.
Thus the odd one goes bananas, finally.
Or a number of stress-related sicknesses
pop up: ulcers, shingles, nervous tics,
alcoholism. It's a strange place.
One guy, Billy, was pulled over by the cops
for going through a stop sign.
The cop climbed into the truck
and was going to ride with Billy to the weigh scales.
Billy, who'd already been acting a little bizarre at work,
freaked out
—driving really fast—
and almost got he and the cop killed.
He had to be picked up by the senior foreman
and ended in the psych ward."

Snow
falling gently, steadily throughout the day.

Alarm clocks that jab into the head
each morning, like so many insane brain surgeons,
the hours that one by one transform themselves
into dollars
while they discreetly, inexorably wear us away,
the emptiness of being controlled by
landlords, mortgage companies,
supervisors,
the insolence of bureaucracies
who are paid to help us,
the abrupt horrifying moment
when after much figuring
it is evident if everything keeps on as it has
there will not be enough money.

"Men and women are also laughing.
I will not tell you what they are laughing at."

      But other
      words
      are passed
      hand to hand
      around the frozen planet,
      thought about, questioned,
      added to:

      the possession and management of the job
      by everyone employed here;
      a fairer method of distributing
      the value of what we produce
      than wages;
      alternate forms of organizing society
      than distant convocations of lawyers and businessmen
      or Party functionaries

      and their generals.

            Run your fingers over
            your newest appliance

or a cup.
When you touch
these
your hands meet the lives of all whose work
brought you this gift.
These are the moments of another's life
there is no possible payment for

—despite those to whom
our existence
is a means to improve themselves:
who ascend from production
into union office or
political office
and vow they will never return to the line.
It is good to escape
to an easier life. But these should not pretend
their prosperity is for us.
They can lie to themselves.
But they do not lessen the cold.

5

Yet if there is a morning without frost,
when a thaw begins,
every location will still have drifts
of dirty snow: each person hurt
and shivering
through this bleak season—
the twisted, the bullies,
those instructed to crawl,
the mad

and those who learned
too much about winter,
who live with it now
as in an unsatisfactory marriage:
unpleasant, bitter, even dangerous
but familiar;

those who adopt the luxury
of not being responsible:
"It's not my fault."
"I only work here."
Why get upset
since it won't do any good
and who am I, anyways?
"It's somebody else's worry."

And should change occur
everyone will not be reasonable.
People out on a Friday night
drinking at a bar—
young men with shirts
fashionably open at the chest
to display thin gold strings around their necks,
young women wearing skirts of whatever length
was recently decreed stylish:
do you think we won't be angry
when we demolish the generals' dream?
Furious at bosses, and at the politicians
of every stripe, who eat our money
and patronize us.
At the men and women of words
who explained and explained
in classrooms, in the papers,
who kept the tricks happening.
Angry at ourselves
once there is nobody else to blame
for errors, harshest with each other
maybe: for one of the tricks is to be well taught
nothing can be improved
and if anyone tries, they're a suckhole
or a fraud. There are no New Women or New Men
to build change, only us
full of fear and rage.

And of accomplishment.
Around us we have created,

we daily create a world
which could be arranged
to let us start work
on the spring.

Yet should change succeed,
in remote mountains, for generations
snow will remain on the highest ridges
and forests
as though on the satellites circling the earth
from which the generals intend to freeze us
below absolute zero.

In Poland
and here
a snowflower
unfolds in the weak sun.

The generals,
traitors
to the human race,
sleep firmly
and dream.

ARBOREAL

When the ocean strikes the shores
of this province, it sends a spray
slapping down on the coast mountains
and valleys: conifers growing eastward
as far as the Rockies.
Here, one range before
the continental divide,
fir and cedar and spruce
stand all winter in the grey rain
and snow.
But each summer, the hills

around the lakeshore are crowded
with visitors
from the plains:
maple and cottonwood and aspen
busy along the roads in the hot mornings
and after sundown. Through these months
the year-round residents
are almost hidden amid the bright green
of spring, and later the autumn colours.
There is even a local tree
influenced by the deciduous species.
Like someone from a nearby town
who keeps a summer home along the Lake,
the larch, technically coniferous,
loses its needles each fall,
blazing yellow
as a dying pine,
and then disappears for the winter
back to Grand Forks or Kelowna—
leaving the November woods
emptier and calmer,
the air in the afternoon carrying only
the slow sigh of the evergreens,
rooted, permanent,
marine.

NUANCE

I was raised
on the north coast mountains
where squalls churn the waves of the inlet
all afternoon, or through a tiny drizzle of mist
in the cove
we rowed one morning over to breakfast
on the calm.

Later, I lived south

in a City where the same rain
takes the tops off the peaks
as it lashes for days at
the sodden port: houses,
trees, even the grass
slick and dripping
under the hills.

But when I moved to the prairie,
the air cleared
and the ground was flat.
"It isn't," people said. "Look again."
And month by month
I decided they were right.
The sky filled and emptied
with a thousand-ship fleet of small clouds
or the giant arc of an approaching front.
The land, as I gazed,
began to roll:
rising to slight bluffs
of aspen and caragana, and descending to
creek-valleys
and shores of the slow rivers.
Everything scaled down
until I could sense elevation
and a falling away
in each field —
earth never completely still
any more than ocean,
both buoyed from underneath
on their own power.

When I returned to the west,
inland,
I was lost in the mountains.
After so much prairie nuance
what happened in this place
seemed overstatement, exaggeration.
If I looked up between the cliffs

that line either side of this valley
I saw only a hole out of a pit.
"No," people told me. "Keep your eyes open."

And ridges appeared
on the forest slopes. I learned where the glaciers
feed the streams, and how these
merge.

The wind
blows the weather along the Lake
past me, carrying the osprey and crow. In summer,
bears drift to the lower ranges for berries
and even in winter, deer beside the highway
where the diesels haul up the grades
break cover for a moment
before plunging back
into the multifarious green.

BREATH: FOR FRED WAH

you know
these mountains breathe
from below   from the valleys:
they breathe in
and Fall
floats down at noon
in the wooded hills
over the Lake
first snow on ridgelines
descends;

breathe out
and Spring
rises from gravel
up the yellowing slopes
between evergreens   the wind
at first with the glaciers in it
and then sun;

                breathe out
sounds of the Lake
flowing against docks
and the rocky shore   air
tosses the willow-tops'
strands and branches   as seaweed
on a choppy day
birch leaves, cottonwood
vibrate
in the breezy light
glints on the moving water—

                the Lake
surges uphill
through the new leaves

you see

COUNTRY FEUDS

Out of town, disagreements between neighbours
are as simple as water:
water rights, diversion of creeks,
water lines
or shared wells that go dry. The feuds
grow naturally as animals:
grazing someone's cows
in return for a spring calf
or whether a quarter of a hog
is equal to a quarter of a heifer
in the fall. Some arguments
root deep in the purpose
of the country: people who want to operate
a small sawmill on their acreage
and the folks across the lane who moved here
for the quiet.

                    Each winter
the troubles become more intense.
Somebody stops speaking to certain friends
whenever they meet in the village
and much later a phone call is made
Hey, are we having a quarrel?
If so, we can really get behind it.
And if not, don't be so surly when we see you.
These winter hassles are not limited
to a few miles of road. Strange letters to officials
—local, regional and national—
get written in the early darkness
on country tables
and mailed.

                    At any season
you must be careful what you say.
Tree farm licences,
road access, ducks' eggs
versus chickens',
when carrots are tastiest and should be picked
—all can be tests. In each home
is a list, continually updated,
of which acquaintances are assets
and which liabilities, what stands on specific issues
are to be condemned.
An outsider or newcomer is allowed a few mistakes
but visitors who persistently express wrong opinions
or inquire too often after a name
currently not mentioned on this property
are subject to classification themselves.

To avoid these disputes
you have to stay in the city. Once you turn off the highway
onto dirt roads
you are headed
for a fight.

SALMONWATER

In this steep region

a bead of rainwater
on a misty day   high above the valleys
drops from a leaf
                    to a small puddle
on the earth
             on which fir needles float
groundwater
            that seeps
to the channels trickling away the glaciers
the snowpack
               becoming
                           stone creeks
pushing boulders down through the forest
coolness
           tributary
of the rivers
widening to lakes
then closing again
                gathering
                      water
  ways out of these mountains
                          power
pulled
        as salmon born inland
oceanward

and later rising
from the Pacific
             to climb
back
into the hills
along the spine of a continent
                   not *this* fish
but the fish
         the creeks

a gift of the sea
and an origin
			returning

WOOD

Back of the highway, in
farmhouse or cabin
men and women can meet,
decide to live together,
have children, grow out of love,
set up strange and unique arrangements
or stay alone
but the winter's wood
has to be cut.
Around these homesteads, in the hills
or along the rivers
the mills and smelter can be thriving
or reduced to one shift a week
but the wood
has to be found
somewhere on the property
or crown land, up old forestry roads
or new microwave access routes.
What the stove requires
must be loaded, trucked to the place,
split and stacked to dry. Pickup, chain saw,
sharpening file, axe:
when the spring snow
has melted enough under the trees
until deep into the fall—
the loud hammering whine
of the saw motor,
the *chunk* and *creak*
of a piece of spruce on the block,
smell of oil
and gasoline. Some people believe

a person's value can be judged
by their woodshed—if this winter's supply
is already stored, you're adequate;
if you have a year's extra
that's better; if two years ahead
you're a success.
But this indicates nothing about quality:
cedar for a fast start, birch for a long burn . . .

As the drifts rise
from first frost to the eaves
the piled fuel
slowly vanishes.
By April, in the sheds
most of the ground is exposed—
covered with the chips, bark
and twigs that proclaim: *time
to get in your wood*

MOTION PICTURES

Of all locations to park, my car prefers
country drive-in theatres:
those fields fenced off in the dusk
echoing with the noise of speakers attached to poles
where every vehicle faces the same way
except a few pickups
containing hardy individuals settled down in the back
under coats and blankets.

                      My car especially enjoys
films about characters on the road
that include travelogue sequences as filler:
shots of strange North American cities
or European landscapes my car will never visit.
My car likes to observe these distant places

without having had to roll that far,
pistons rising and plunging,
all systems functioning, alert
for any failure.
What my car isn't happy about
are chase scenes: vehicles smashing
together, or swerving onto sidewalks
or down embankments to end in flames.
My car has passed too many overturned trucks
and police flares at other accidents
to successfully remind itself this is just a movie.
And my car seems indifferent
if the plot involves only people
indoors. But when this occurs
it loves to look higher than the screen
and the hills around,
up at the massed stars,
and recollect certain nights
it spent away out on the earth
in gear and travelling.

                       My car is always a little regretful
when the films conclude
and it has to get in line
down the usual hard highway.

THE TOWN WHERE TIME TAKES HIS HOLIDAYS

In a town with only one mill
everybody monitors the mill's health
eager to prescribe remedies
for any problems, actual or imaginary.
People agree this town doesn't *depend*
on the mill: there's always tourism.
But visitors can be elusive, whereas the mill
stays in its lumberyard

oblivious to a wet spring
or early snow.

Yet one tourist
who regularly visits here
is Time. The buildings along the main street
are largely unchanged since just after the town began
in 1897. Time finds this attractive
for when he is on holidays
age stands still.
One summer he didn't appear
and the civic fathers erected a shopping mall.
Then he was seen in the streets again
and the aldermen proposed restoration
of a stern-wheeler used on the Lake
before the highway went through.

Time relishes
the slow pace in town, how people stop to talk
in stores. He loves to chat with men and women
in to shop from the Slocan
who homesteaded during the 1960s
and who preserve that era. And Time is pleased
to speak with their neighbours, Doukhobors
who first settled in 1908
and who maintain *their* customs.
When Time is downtown
people discover a nickel in the parking meter
lasts all day.

Nobody elderly dies
as long as Time is around. The only part of his job
he continues with while fishing on the Lake
or relaxing in the lounge at the Heritage Inn
concerns children: they are so impatient to be older
he doesn't have the heart to deny them.

And like a resident, Time hears
about the mill. He knows

what he does is bought and sold there.
A mill employee he meets on the boat rental dock
describes the work:
the new guys live for the coffee breaks,
the young guys live for the weekends, and the old-timers
live for their vacations.
Yet should the mill be modernized or
left as is, shut down to save the forests
or expanded to improve the local economy?
Time listens to the town's opinions
but insists he is off duty
and refuses to express what he believes.

BROKEN TOES

David McFadden, the poet, is fascinated
by coincidences. For example, he might write about
a friend of his who recently
broke a toe, and would you believe it is the very same toe
on the very same foot
David McFadden had broken years before
when his wife was in hospital having their daughter Alison
or maybe his daughter Jennifer?
I'm pretty sure it was Alison, however, because
the friend whose toe was broken also has a daughter
named Jennifer (except he spells it Jenefer for some reason)
and that extra coincidence is exactly
what David McFadden notices
so I'm convinced he would have mentioned this
in conversation about the incident
unless possibly he didn't because of the different spellings.

Another coincidence is that I,
who am writing about David McFadden,
for two years shared an office with him
when we both taught in Nelson, British Columbia.
I used to insist what he thought were wonderful coincidences

actually were silly accidents
but for the purposes of this poem I'll call it a coincidence
that he and I cordially occupied room 313
of St. Martin's Hall at David Thompson University Centre
and even shared a typewriter, though they gave us separate phones.
Perhaps they meant to imply that we write alike
(after all, isn't both our material chopped-up prose?)
but that we have different things to say.
In fact, he and I decided to disagree on almost every point
about writing, but reached harmonious concurrence
with regard to some people active in the literary scene
whom we both despise. Their names will be revealed to you
if you send a stamped, self-addressed envelope
to room 313, St. Martin's Hall, David Thompson University Centre,
Nelson, B.C. And if by coincidence
both David McFadden and I are back for a visit
and you happen at the time to have broken the precise toe
which David McFadden and his friend broke
(you have to state in a covering letter which toe it is)
we'll send you the list of names.
Of course you can lie about the toe
but then you have to guess which toe is the correct one.

Now, you might not care to possess these names
or about the business of the broken toes.
I personally couldn't imagine why anyone would want to know
about either, and particularly the latter. But David McFadden

just smiles at that thought, and begins, "Well, ther. . .".
After which he goes "A-hem," sort of clearing his throat,
as he does whenever he's about to deliver himself
of a necessary but difficult pronouncement
such as pointing out the foolish behaviour of some administrators
to them, or when in class
he wishes to praise what a student has written
and yet wants to demonstrate a few serious errors
—as he sees it—in pronoun reference or character motivation
or theme. "A-hem," he goes again,
"if you're not interested in these things

what *does* mean a lot to you? Make a list
of everything you care about, that really matters.
Better yet, be sure you always write about what's important to you.
That's what I do," says David McFadden.

STUDENTS

The freshman class-list printouts
showed birthdates so recent
Wayman was sure the computer was in error.
One young man, however, was curious
about Wayman's mention near the start of term
of his old college newspaper:
"You were an editor *when*? Wow,
that's the year I was born."

The wisdom of the students
hadn't altered, though.
Wayman observed many clung to
The Vaccination Theory of Education
he remembered: once you have had a subject
you are immune
and never have to consider it again.
Other students continued to endorse
The Dipstick Theory of Education:
as with a car engine, where as long as the oil level
is above the add line
there is no need to put in more oil,
so if you receive a pass or higher
why put any more into learning?

At the front of the room, Wayman sweated
to reveal his alternative.
"Adopt The Kung Fu Theory of Education,"
he begged.
"Learning as self-defence. The more you understand
about what's occurring around you
the better prepared you are to deal with difficulties."

The students remained skeptical.
A young woman was a pioneer
of The Easy Listening Theory of Learning:
spending her hours in class
with her tape recorder earphones on,
silently enjoying a pleasanter world.
"Don't worry, I can hear you,"
she reassured Wayman
when after some days he was moved to inquire.

Finally, at term's end
Wayman inscribed after each now-familiar name on the list
the traditional single letter.
And whatever pedagogical approach
he or the students espoused,
Wayman knew this notation would be pored over
with more intensity
than anything else Wayman taught.

WHY YOU ONLY GOT "B PLUS"

During the 1950s, we believed
the world's supply of "A"s was inexhaustible.
If a student satisfactorily completed
—the argument went—
everything asked of her or him
that was worth an "A". Wasn't this the utmost
requested of the student, so didn't they deserve
the highest grade?

But a few people foresaw difficulties.
From time to time a journalist
or educational theoretician or mining engineer
warned in *Reader's Digest* or at a PTA meeting
that this practice courted disaster,
that we really didn't know enough about

proven reserves of the letter.
And as the Earth's available stock of "A"s
finally was understood to be limited
our attitudes changed.

Yet there is no agreement
on how to cope with the problem.
The government maintains
imports should be controlled
while lessening domestic use.
Some observers counter, however,
the international shortfall is artificial,
designed to increase the power
of those who govern the supply.
They speak of boatloads of "A"s
deliberately kept offshore.
Other experts think the government's program
is good, as it reduces people's dependence
on external vicissitudes
while encouraging self-reliance.
But different commentators declare
the wealthy can always obtain "A"s
while the majority suffer. Others state
the restrictions on this grade
will help the battle against inflation.

Despite the controversy
various stopgap measures have been introduced.
Besides the cancellation
of delivery of "A"s to arbitrary areas
—for example, classes that meet between
eight and nine a.m.,
the bell curve scheme
has been widely adopted.
Here, a sort of Procrustean graph
is lowered onto the pages of a mark-book
ensuring only a minimum of precious "A"s
need to be released.

Long term solutions? Certain educators are confident
technology will provide the answer.
Then there are terrorists
who say they hope a system without "A"s
will create a climate for not having "B"s
and eventually for eliminating grades completely.
In any case, the best estimates
of the planet's "A" resources
are greater than was recently thought
though definitely finite.
So it doesn't appear
we will escape shortages and rationing.
But we do have many years
to solve our dilemma
before the world's last "A"
in China or someplace
flows out of somebody's marking pen.

WAYMAN AMONG THE ADMINISTRATORS

After some years of teaching
Wayman discovered that the gentle moss of administration
formerly coating the tree of knowledge
had transformed itself into a virulent fungus.
Memos from financial vice-presidents and
deputy service managers
began to cover Wayman's desk
like spores. These contained phrases such as
"educational delivery systems"
as if the college was a cartage and storage enterprise
or perhaps a railroad. Also present were terms like
"cost-effectiveness per student-hour"—
a figure apparently obtainable by reading the dials
implanted into the skull of each enrollee during registration.

Meanwhile, a froth of busyness
emanated from the front office

as carpenters and electricians rebuilt adjoining classrooms
into more cubicles for freshly hired personnel
deemed necessary to oversee the dwindling number of courses offered
due to the lack of funds available for public education.

And the newcomers established themselves
by memo. "We're having trouble identifying people
by the two initials they've been using on internal communications,"
one circular read. "Henceforth all memos
must be signed by *three* initials.
Please memo me back indicating
the three initials you will use."

The campus director, a man from the old days,
attempted feverishly to match his superiors' and inferiors' memos
with messages of his own. One Monday Wayman arrived at work
to receive a note from the director duly routed
to all administrative, teaching and support staff
which read in its entirety: "Good morning."

When managerial functions were reorganized yet again
and the ratio climbed dangerously closer to
an administrator for each faculty member
Wayman concluded maybe these men and women were right.
Perhaps the job here really did depend on
them holding meetings with each other
and writing up the results of such gatherings for circulation.
Never one to stand in the way of progress
Wayman sat down at his typewriter on a spring afternoon
and produced a memo he hoped was equal
to any issued that day.
"I," Wayman wrote,
"quit."

UPLANDS

I broke out of timber
after some hours
onto a meadow
rising along a slope
—grass and some rocks
and stumps,

but as I entered, I was conscious of
bears; in smaller clearings
before this, perhaps by a creek
into my sight
plodded the bear, newly out of the den
in May, for instance, too much snow
on the higher ranges, searching for food
here: the animal
not hostile,
concerned with its own affairs
but

    a threat
impossible to predict
with a history of sudden
overwhelming force,
large as a grave

—a presence, a chance
near me
crossing an open space
about noon

EAST KOOTENAY ILLUMINATION

As I drove in summer along the valley
between the Purcells and the high wall of the Rockies,
the road speeding north through forests
and out to broad vistas of lakes or heights of land

I heard the earth

tell me: when you know the blue of the sky
does not extend to the sun,
when you feel *there is the star we swing around*
blazing this morning above the apparent horizon,

you sense that this planet, this white-and-blue ball
turning through space
watches what happens
with benign indifference.
Formed of matter which originated
immense distances away, the earth
is intrigued to see what occurs in its interior
or on its surface,
wishes all living beings well,
yet is unconcerned. Much is at stake
for any species, but not for the world.
That which humans find beautiful, and threaten,
the earth does not treasure. Atoms
are what are marvellous to the planet:
the atmosphere can carry smoke, lose oxygen,
allow more ultraviolet in, fill with radioactive dust,
the globe remains whole; pollution or species death
is merely a rearrangement of molecules
and not a loss. The earth observes
as if it attends a play, unmoved by
the outcome, although it wants the actors to succeed
because of its friendly nature.
"Thrive, thrive," the earth says,
its only law, and if a species proves unstable
or destructive, another will replace it

or won't. This is still a world
if it rolls lifeless around the sun —
the planet remembers when its atmosphere
was nitrogen and carbon dioxide
before photosynthesizing organisms
appeared; it remembers when it had no atmosphere.
And when in some cataclysm the globe
disperses back to interstellar space,
these atoms had their time as this planet, as the earth,
as they had their time before in stars.

And as I steered north
on an artificially hardened surface
in the valley of the rivers we call Kootenay and Columbia,
I felt that always with me is the earth
like a friend too remote
to assist in any difficulty
but interested to learn
what I will accomplish:

myself, a person,
human beings,

and the third planet from a star.

SAVING THE WORLD

They had just tied up the tug at Creston
he said, secured the logs at the booming ground
under the bridge. They heard a cry
as though from an animal
in trouble. And again.
He got the boom boat driver
and they turned on the searchlight
and cast off to see what it was.

In the beam of the lamp, they found
someone had thrown a dog from the bridge,

a pup whose muzzle had been tied shut
so tightly its teeth
had been driven into the bleeding flesh
of the mouth. Its forepaws were crossed
and bound hard together with rope
and its back legs also were lashed together.
But the dog had survived the fall,
terrified, barely able to make a sound,
bobbing on the water alongside the boom, head up
then head under. They backed the boat closer
but their wash drove the animal below the surface
once more, and when he fished it out
and slashed through the wet cords
its eyes went flat and rigid
and it died. And he said
he stood cursing, knife in his hand
anyone who could treat a dog like this
would do the same to a child or woman
or a helpless man.

         And as he told me of his rage
I remembered this sailor's grief
for his own children
lost twice in the ruptured tubes
of his wife,
and my children
lost in abortion and
indecision, and
thought it for the best.
Then I recalled his anger
that the world needs,
that has to be passed on.

So much left to do.

The tortured dog on the deck.

MONASHEE

After supper, he aims the pickup
past the woodlot where the cows graze
under the pines, along the dirt road
to the meadows in the forest
near the top of the hills.
Here he keeps his horses. In the back of the truck,
besides an old set of coveralls from work
in case he must repair fencing,
he has loaded his saddle and tack,
freshly oiled.

            When he arrives
he calls over and inspects
the gelding, then the mare.
But he doesn't ride.
He stands thinking of the skidder
they brought in at four
he has to fix tomorrow.
Then he has to check the hydraulics on the Cat.
The evenings are light
this late in June, the dark animals
rest against the trees,
while above him the sky
crossed by white clouds
is blue,
the colour of hope.

THE FACE OF JACK MUNRO

THE HANDS

While the person at the podium speaks
the hands of the audience lift
to touch chins,
lips,
the undersides of the nose.
Fingers thus lie across mouths
as if to stifle a shriek
of boredom, or some comment
on the words being ceaselessly launched into the air.
Perhaps the hands
want to bar the words
from entering the body. Yet sounds
do not enter through the face
but through our ears.

As the voice continues
bodies begin to slump in their seats
as if pressed by an invisible force
of custom or obligation. Or they sag
because despite these hands
the words find their way inside
and settle,
dragging us down.

MEETING

Two hundred mammals pack the room, finding seats
or standing along the walls. They chitter and hum
as they circulate to greet each other, gesture,
discuss the situation. In front at some tables
rest a dozen heavy reptiles
whose decision the mammals are here to direct
if they can. With the reptiles are
a few mammals
anxious to serve these masters, to sound like them,

hoping eventually to be awarded scales
and be allowed to doze all afternoon in the sun.

When the other mammals line up to speak
at the microphone, the reptiles stare impassively
or swivel their eyes to regard the delegations
the speakers say they represent.
The mammals growl or chirp
about fur, about warmth,
about the sweetness of honey.
As they talk, occasionally a reptile tongue flickers out
tasting other news.
"We are here on behalf of the young ones, the babies
born alive and needing nurture,"
a mammal at the microphone cries.
But if any reptile is hearing these words
it thinks: *Eggs? What do eggs require?*

When the mammals at last are silent
some of the reptiles stir.
"Face reality," one explains
to the hairy things crowding the hall.
"Blood is cold.
You may not like it, we may not like it
but it is a fact. Nature is not capable of supporting
the activities you suggest.
We are charged by authority to administer
within realistic limits.
We have no choice but to turn down your proposal
in your best interests. The means to provide what you want
are just not available."

After the vote
the reptiles ponderously exit
trailed by the mammals they have tamed.
The others remain here
barking and arguing, cursing and
planning, still
determined.

BEETLE

As the room
is called to order
we form
a large
overturned beetle
its legs thrashing
clumsily at air:
most people present
want to resolve
matters honestly
cleanly
yet
at one side of the room
a person talks too
glibly, this other person
displays a few effective tricks
of speech, most of us
say nothing
and however we vote
decide afterwards
whether to participate
further
The head
of this insect
struggling
to right itself
often has its own
scheme
for how the rest here
should heave ourselves
erect
it resents
or tries to deflect
other plans
Meanwhile time
is made a limit: how long
we can stay interested

or the availability
of the room
or other meetings
some say they must
attend next

Now and then the beetle's back
does scrape forward
by inches along
the floor, its feet
pushing and slipping, then
catching
Most of us here
would like a better
means of locomotion
but so far
those with ideas
to speed our passage
too often have proved
betrayers or
tyrants
so we continue
this
democratic
crawl

THE FACE OF JACK MUNRO

1

In the November rain we walked
back and forth
across a driveway which led
to a parking lot:
four of us—two support staff,
two faculty—and we stood aside,
dripping, if a car tried to nose in past us
or emerged. The wet wind
chilled our faces
and hands, as we paced
on the asphalt flowing with a thin wash
of runoff, so a clamminess
also rose into our soaked boots.
Cardboard signs
that hung from our neck with string
were wrapped in clear plastic
down which the water rolled, while we held them
against the gusts of the storm.
Once somebody from the main entrance
showed up with a bag of doughnuts
a supporter had donated
and Dale volunteered to go for coffees
which we eventually drank,
holding the hot styrofoam cups
in our hands. The rain
seeped through the seams of my coat
after a while, dampening my shirt
and then my skin. In the culvert
under the driveway
the water sang, pouring through
into a ditch
lined with tall weeds and grasses,
some paper litter,
in the cold rain.

2

I worked that autumn with Dale
Zieroth, Maureen Shaw,
John Waters, John Reed
and others—just names to you,
probably. All of us were employed
to instruct
what we knew.

But those who adminstered us
and those who had hired
them
wanted us to know
only a prescribed amount.
We were not to notice
that in the air
a sour odour
was leaking, as if from a refinery
upwind. It was a stench
of sulphur, of worn dollar bills,
of half-digested steak
belched through false smiles
at the poor.

After a while, everyone smelled it.
Some pretended it wasn't there.

3

This stink
arose from fear.
One gang of liars
had been elected, and to them
our lives were mirrors:
they saw evil.
So they strode into welfare dentists' offices
and shut these down.

They ordered the demolition
of wheelchair access ramps
and their replacement by stairs.
They informed battered women
fortitude is a virtue.
They advised the young without jobs
to eat less.
They ordered tenants
to register with a central bureau
so files could be opened on our suitability
to be housed.
They said discrimination of any type
is acceptable
as long as no harm is intended.
They announced everyone paid by the public
except themselves
could be fired without cause.

They put a price on the highways
and handed these over to their friends.
They evaluated the firehalls
and the hospitals for the retarded
and offered these in the bond markets
of the East. They enforced an embargo
on food allocated to the hungry
and paid for enormous scaffoldings
to be erected in the largest cities
for purposes no one could fathom.
They told civic officials
their jurisdictions would henceforth be limited
to bird inventories and traffic signal maintenance.
And that these functions
would be assigned
to a select list of corporations.
They invited purchasers to submit bids
on clearing the wolves and elk from our forests.
They advised farmers
there is no crop more vital to human need
than mortgages.

Whatever was owned in common
they closed, ruined, or gave away.
Our trees could not be cut and milled quickly enough,
so they issued permits for logs
to be dragged directly overseas.
This was still too slow: they gave grants
to research companies
to investigate the towing of whole coastal islands
offshore for processing.
Money witheld from schools
went to fund extra tracking of railroads
to haul ore more rapidly to dumps by the ocean.
When customers balked
at taking entire mountains for free
a program was initiated to offer compensation
for the removal of these detriments to the environment.
The government announced their intention
to sell the rivers, sell streams,
sell the water still in the clouds.
And they introduced tax increases
to pay the costs of implementing
these measures.

4

But we drew a line
and walked it.

First there were rallies and marches—
forty thousand of us
making a giant stadium pulse and hum
with protest, banners, shouts
and leaflets.
And strange events
resulted: other liars, who had always claimed
at election time to be on our side
vanished
leaving only their campaign posters
which they asked us to erect on our lawns

in four or five years
if there were still candidates and elections.
At our union meetings, now
disunity
was general. Some were opposed
to any action, others
demanded it;
some were terrified of changes
we might make,
others of the changes already decreed.

Yet women and men
stood one by one
and spoke
and we argued and
voted
and together we constructed a line.

So the union executives
had to announce a Plan:
little by little, they said,
groups of us could emerge
and stand in the rain.

Tens of thousands of us
that November
did—the clerks who issue government
liquor permits, the bridge crews
from the Highways yards,
maintenance people from colleges,
teachers of physical education
and French, data processors
from the government insurance bureaus.

While we grew
the newspapers and televisions
appeared frantic: they hired extra scribblers
to be sure every person who wished to cross our line

was interviewed in depth.
Columns and editorials
brayed about chaos
but eighty thousand human beings
now stood outside their workplace
and not a rock was thrown,
not a single tire slashed,
nobody even complained of being shoved.

Yet there were those
who pushed past us
into the empty buildings.
Not many did this
and in some places none,
but some.

No one called them scabs.
A scab is a crust of dead matter
in a wound. These people were
leeches, desperate to suck nourishment for themselves
from a stricken host, leeches
scurrying to live
in an open sore,
leeches unwilling to join,
to help their neighbours
but eager to share our gains
if we won.

And after two weeks
we began to win.
The people drenched on the line
learned to laugh at the sneering
of the television, refused to believe any more
in the newspaper,
trusted each other and the words of approval
from additional citizens who arrived each morning
to walk beside us.
The politicians and news teams

became increasingly frenzied,
they found economists to forecast
the end of the earth,
on our line
people almost burst into song.

The frightened among us
redoubled their efforts:
"Let's accept the situation. The smell
will disappear in time." Or:
"Let's find a perfume—new words
to describe what they are doing to us
that don't stink so badly."

But by the second Sunday,
poised to go out
were others of us:
the next day, municipal parks board employees,
drivers of garbage trucks, drainage
inspectors, and later the same week
the men and women who staff the cafeterias
on the coastal ferries
and the deckhands, bus drivers
and those who repair transit vehicles
and clean them, and some days after that
all but a designated core of hospital workers.

The world was full of love.

5

In our midst, though,
was error
greater than the leeches:
a cancer
few could see.

At this hour
in history, when it was clear to anyone

that our daily work
enables the world to function, and who
are parasites

there arose

a man called Jack Munro

—a burly man,
elected to represent the roar
and hustle of the sawmills, of the plywood
and fibreboard plants, the horns and machine-noise
of the logging sidehills, a man
come into the quiet offices
of the union, the structures
that whispered to him
power,
the rooms where bargains are made
by shirts and ties,
the conference corridors
where lives are traded;

—this man
eaten inside by the invisible cancer
now suddenly shouldered past
those who had claimed they were leading us.
He whistled for a government aircraft
which arrived for him that Sunday,
and he soared
high over the rock-firm picket lines,
far above the panic filling the thoughts
of owners and company vice-presidents and personnel managers,
away up beyond our certain success.
And when Jack Munro descended
he entered the Kelowna house
of the man who headed
this government of death.

And the two men shook hands, because this other man

was also very sick with the cancer.
Then Jack Munro
took out his wallet
and placed it on a table.

The other man
took out his wallet, too,
and placed it beside Munro's.
The leather cases
were almost identical,
each thick with crisp bills
and uncashed cheques.
And while Jack Munro sat
and stuffed snacks into his fat jowls,
the two wallets
commenced negotiations.
Both wallets agreed
the moment was perilous,
that authority must be maintained
and that for this to occur
one side must win and the other lose.
They agreed
the present actions of the many
in daring to resist
were more dangerous to authority
than the actions of the few in oppressing.
So it was concluded
that Jack Munro was to order the hierarchy below him
to close down our lines,
that in return for nothing
Jack Munro was to announce our defeat,
to inform us we had obtained through our efforts
nothing.

And in return for our compliance
the government would be free
to implement whatever it desired.
But we should be grateful

because at least
the usual authority would be preserved.

And the mouths of the two wallets smiled,
and the two wallets shook hands
for the news photographers
and Jack Munro was carried again
high into the atmosphere
from where he started to issue his commands

and now we saw the cancer,
saw how deep the cancer had spread
among us,
and were told Jack Munro's orders
were non-debatable by us,
were told voting by us on this issue
was irrelevant

and we did not know what to do
and we were lost.

6

Thus Jack Munro
sold out the woodyard
by the creek, sold out the school bus
letting the children off by the lane
up to a ranch, sold out the waiting room
at Emergency, the empty job boards
at the employment centres.
Jack Munro sold out
the regional museum,
the women and men anxious
for an opening at daycare,
sold out the grapple operator
on the landing, sold out the secretaries
headed for lunch, the gill netters, instrument
technicians, welders
and geologists.

He sold out the palsied
and the athlete, sold out the accountant at her desk
and the man wild in the street
who knows he has lost control.

Jack Munro sold out this province
house by house,
district by district,
kilometre by kilometre.

7

How could it occur
that direction of our struggle
shrank to one man?
How is it we took up the fight
convinced of the good will of those
we put above us?

> Those days in November I felt
> the presence of
> another room alongside this one,
> another field and sky
> beside this meadow
> and air.
> It seemed we had built
> a passageway to that crystal life,
> a door which took shape
> from our careful daily acts of
> defiance.
> But we left a few to keep
> that opening for us
> and when we tried to cross through
> we learned they had taken it away.

What Jack Munro accomplished
now hangs over every hour.
At each press conference
to explain the curtailment of more liberties

the government spokesperson stares at us
with the eyes
of Jack Munro.
At the bargaining sessions
where negotiators from management
demand we be punished, earn less,
live less well,
the employers' representatives speak
using the voice
of Jack Munro.
The supervisor delivering layoff notices,
the tribunal refusing to hear the eviction appeal,
the businessmen and women gloating over dinner
at the news of the reduction of
payments to the single unemployed
—all share a face
puffy with greed and fright and satisfaction,
the face of
Jack Munro.

> A malignancy
> bitter and deep
> has carved a bully's cunning
> into the convolutions of Jack Munro's brain.
> But the spores that brought him this tumour,
> this anti-democracy, this fear
> originated elsewhere
> and have taken some root
> in us, too.
> How else can we forget each time
> that decisions must be made by ourselves
> and not left to the leaderships,
> officers,
> steering committees?
> For centuries
> this cancer has taught us to obey,
> spoken for us, told us what to think.

Yet we have always

breathed
on our own, at least.
And our emancipation
is as natural
and complex
as that simple motion:
inhale
        exhale
bringing the life that is oxygen
to the blood
bearing away the wastes

like injustice,
which other living things
transform into their wholesome existences.
So there is a use
even for a great wrong
on this planet
in this process
of mutual
and perfect
solidarity
we still have to devise

for ourselves.

IN THE TRAITORS' SEASON

The welfare minister orders cuts
in each monthly payment by
what for her
is the price of one working lunch.
These are the dollars
on which people have to eat for a week
or more. The minister's eyes are
empty and flat
as the soleplate of an iron, the iron

which scorched her eyes
when she went into business
when she began to feel she had to fire someone
never could dress as she wanted.
All one cheque day
two of us stand outside a welfare office
collecting names on a petition to appeal.
Not one signature
becomes a cheese sandwich or a bag of onions.

The education minister
refuses to agree to a plan
one school board has devised. Their idea
would protect the jobs
of teachers and custodians threatened by layoffs
caused by a transfer of government funds
to a ski resort developer.
When the minister gives his reasons
deep in the pit of his open mouth
somebody is strapping a small boy
hard, because he was late for school again
because there was no one to wake him in time.

The premier
appoints an important distributor of pornography
to head a six-month international exposition.
At a kitchen table across my city
a man puts down his fork
and tells his wife he is leaving her.

Family life is important to the premier.
He stays alone in a hotel
two blocks from the legislative building.
He works late, only rarely gives an interview
to the press, has just had installed
a stairway from his office to the cabinet meeting room
so he can attend sessions of his cabinet
without having to enter any public corridors.
From his hotel bed, the premier dreams

he is a cloud floating high over his province.
He permits sunshine
to pour down into a golden valley.
Now he is angered: lightning
smites his enemy.

A carpenter stares at the dispatch board.
Eighty per cent of his local
without jobs. It will be sixteen months
before his name rises
to be eligible for the next call.
But he knows the members employed by firms
constructing a new rapid transit guideway
work overtime every afternoon and most
weekends. In his heart
the man enters a storefront
run by the jobless as a drop-in.
His clothes are stained with mud
from a few hours labour he managed to obtain
this morning. He asks if we are aware of
any strikes. "I can usually get hired
if the company is still operating,"
he says.

One woman on the picket line
at an office equipment plant
worked here fifteen years
before the new manager
decided he could break the union.
As negotiations began this time
the company locked her out
to spend nine months on the sidewalk
watching the traffic crawl into the city every morning
and return each afternoon. Head office
has approved a budget item
for extra fencing, security guards, additional salary
for supervisors, fees for lawyers
to secure and enforce injunctions
and for recruiting non-union employees.

In good weather
the woman brings with her
the folding garden chair she bought
for her narrow apartment balcony.

In her building, a man takes down his shotgun
and begins to fire from his window
into the street of the poor.
A half hour later, the police
in position outside
he turns the weapon so the barrel
points toward his face.

While the young who have work
and who don't
sit in the bars where the jukebox sings of love
again and again, love
about which the young know so little
and feel much.

                    The rest of us
stand rigid as trees
far back in the mountains
under deep snow, scarcely
breathing, enduring, our boughs
brought in close to the trunk
under the weight of the snow
the only motion in the icy forest
imperceptible, as when a branch
finds the snow at last too heavy
and gives up a bit more
so some snow
chutes off in a rush
leaving a white powder hanging in the air
for an instant
after the sound
then everything is as it was

as though waiting
to hear
from nowhere
and every place
the start of a red
and black
laughter
like the first faint touch
of moving air
which will begin
which is all that can begin
the thaw

In memoriam: Joan Partridge Crocker.

ACKNOWLEDGEMENTS

Poems here have been published in or accepted for: *This Magazine; Saturday Night; Waves; Matrix; Poetry Australia; The Fiddlehead; The Tamarack Review; The Little Magazine; The Harbor Review; Event; Convergence; BC Monthly; The Canadian Forum; The Nation; Queen's Quarterly; Cafeteria; Labour/ Le Travailleur; The Minnesota Review; Speaking Out; Anthropology of Work Review; Colorado State Review; The Ontario Review; Canadian Literature; West Coast Review; Writing; Zest; The University of Windsor Review.* "Paper" appeared in *Poetry;* "Mike," "Country Feuds," and "Motion Pictures" appeared in *The Hudson Review;* "Lecture," "Why You Only Got 'B Plus'," and "The Hands" first appeared in *TriQuarterly,* a publication of Northwestern University.

In addition, "Job Security" was issued as a broadside by the Vancouver Industrial Writers' Union in April, 1983. "The Drawer" was broadcast on CBC Radio's *Morningside* program September 5, 1983. Other poems here were broadcast on CBC Radio's *Anthology* program. Thanks to the Canada Council for a Short Term Grant in the autumn of 1982, which gave me time for some of these poems. The title "Articulating West" is from the book of criticism by W.H. New; the section title *Opusculum Paedagogum* is from the poem "A Study of Two Pears" by Wallace Stevens.